2023 GLUTEN FREE BUYERS GUIDE

2023
GLUTEN FREE
BUYERS GUIDE

Discover the ultimate list of
community-voted top products that
will make your mouth water

JOSH SCHIEFFER

Table of Contents

How to Read

Example: Breakfast-On-The-Go

2023 Annual Gluten Free Awards

1st Place Winner: Canyon Bakehouse Honey Whole Grain English Muffins

2nd Place Winner: Schär Cinnamon Raisin Bagels

3rd Place Winner: Goodie Girl Cookies® Blueberry Breakfast Biscuits

Runner Up:

Bobo's Banana Peanut Butter Protein Bar

Other Great Products:

Bakery On Main Organic Probiotic Walnut Banana Premium Oatmeal

Glutino English Muffins

Introduction

This happens to be our ninth Gluten Free Buyers Guide and our 14th year hosting the Annual Gluten Free Awards. If you are not familiar with the book, I thought it would be best to explain what the book is and more importantly what it is not.

This book is much more than a list of great gluten free products to buy, we also list some of the best gluten free personalities. Being on a gluten free diet can be isolating in so many ways. With a heavy emphasis on celiac disease, we produce eye opening information gathered from polling our readers. Our goal is to ensure you do not feel so alone.

This book does not contain every single gluten free product available in every market. The gluten free industry has changed dramatically since we started in 2008. Virtually no regional grocery chains had private label gluten free products and now it is the norm with west coast chains like Safeway and east coast chains like Publix. We tend to focus on brands with national distribution and national grocery chains. We do this so you have access to these products regardless of where you live. Oftentimes ordering online can save you money, time and widen your options dramatically.

You will not find every brand or product listed in this book on your local grocery shelves. It's a strange fact to some but often brands have to pay to sit on the shelves of most grocery stores. This is especially true for products that don't get purchased as often, like gluten free products. If you have a favorite product that your store doesn't carry, you can request that they stock it for a trial period. If it sells, more than likely they will keep it without the brand paying for the space. However, if a competing brand buys out the shelf space your product will more than likely disappear. This is the cold hard truth about the industry. Those of us who eat gluten free food to maintain a healthy lifestyle pay the price. Gluten Free food is our medicine for a diagnosis we didn't want or ask for. Please use this guide to help make your gluten free lifestyle the best it can be.

Why do I tell you all of this? Those of us with restricted diets have limited options especially in rural parts of the country. I do not want your diet and the products you eat being dictated by what brands pay to sit on your local shelves. The product placement in your local store is not based on how great the product is and how well it tastes. If you want to have the best gluten free products in your pantry, more than likely you will need to travel to multiple stores and order online.

At the end of the day, I want you to know that there are great gluten free products for you and your family. If you are new to the gluten free diet or just struggling to maintain the diet because of product availability or poor product quality, we published this book for you.   Please read "Our Story" so you have a better understanding of why we have hundreds of product pictures and not just a list of a million random gluten free products.

This year we had nearly 2,000 people take part in the voting process. The individual responses are all rolled up in the following pages. We added a few new gluten free award categories and have organized the book in sections for easier navigation.

Our Story

The story behind The Gluten Free Awards that very few people know

I remember it like it was yesterday when my four-year-old son Jacob, now eighteen, was playing in the kiddie pool with other kids that I assumed were his age based on their height. After asking all the surrounding kids what ages they were, I realized Jacob was significantly smaller than kids his own age. This prompted my wife and I to seek a professional opinion. After consulting with our family physician, she confirmed that Jacob had essentially stopped growing for an entire year without us realizing it. He was referred to Jeff Gordon's Children's Hospital in Charlotte North Carolina to discuss possible growth hormone therapy. The doctors there reviewed Jacob's case and requested a few blood tests based on some suspicions they had.

Our cell phone service at our house was terrible so when the doctor finally called with the blood results, my wife and I ran to the front of the driveway to hear the doctor clearly. With a sporadic signal, we heard "Jacob has celiac disease." We looked at each other as tears ran down my wife's face. We huddled closer to the phone and asked, "what is celiac disease?". After getting a brief description mixed with crappy cell service and happy neighbors waving as they drove by, my wife and I embraced and wept. We were told to maintain his normal diet until we could have an endoscopy and biopsy for further confirmation. Once confirmed our next visit was to a registered dietitian for guidance.

Jayme, my wife, made the appointment and called me with a weird request. "Will you meet me at the dietitian's house for a consultation?". I was confused when she said to go to her house. Jayme then explained that the dietician's daughter had celiac disease too and the best way to show the new lifestyle to patients would be to dive right in. I'll admit, it was a bit uncomfortable at first to be in a strangers' house looking at their personal items but looking back now, I wouldn't change it for the world. That encounter is ultimately the motivation behind The Gluten Free Awards and the associated Gluten Free Buyers Guide. We left her house with complete understanding of cross contamination, best practices and what products they personally liked and disliked. We new what the product packaging looked like and is the reason we have so many product images in the guide. That visit was life changing and left us feeling confident as we made our way to the local health food store.

That first trip shopping took forever. Each label was read, and cross checked with our list of known gluten containing suspects. It was also shocking to see the bill when it was time to pay. We had replaced our entire pantry and fridge with all products that had the "Gluten Free" label. We both worked full-time and had decent paying jobs and it still set us back financially.

We looked for support groups locally and came across a "100% Gluten-Free Picnic" in Raleigh, which was two hours away from where we lived. This was our first time meeting other people with celiac disease and we were fortunate to have met some informative people that were willing to help with the hundreds of questions we had. We were introduced to a family whose son had been recently diagnosed with celiac disease as well. His condition was much worse than Jacobs and he was almost hospitalized before finally being diagnosed. They confided in us as we shared similar stories. There were two differences that would change my life forever. The first was the fact that they didn't have the same experience with a registered dietitian. Instead, they were handed a two-page Xerox copy of "safe foods". Second, they didn't have the financial security to experiment with gluten free counterparts. Their first two months exposed to the gluten free lifestyle left them extremely depressed and broke.

On our way home from that picnic, Jayme and I felt compelled to help make a difference in some way. We were determined to help that family and others being diagnosed with this disease. Up until that day, we hadn't found a resource that gave unbiased opinions on gluten free products and services. Fast forward a few years and I too was diagnosed with celiac disease. That year, The Gluten Free Awards were born.

Originally our vision was to create a one-page website with a handful of categories organized by peoples' favorites. Since 2010 we have produced The Annual Gluten Free Awards (GFA) growing into over sixty gluten free categories. After several requests, in 2014, we took the GFA results and published our first Gluten Free Buyers Guide. The annual guide is sold primarily in the United States however we continue to see increased global sales. Each year we have people vote for their favorite gluten free products and we now communicate to nearly 25,000 people weekly through our email list.

We want to thank those special people and organizations that brought us to where we are today:

Pat Fogarty MS, RD, LDN for allowing us to enter your home.

Jeff Gordon's Children's Hospital

Raleigh Celiac Support Groups

Dean Meisel, MD, FAAP for the excellent medical care he provides for our family.

I hope you have learned something new from the story behind The Gluten Free Awards. Today, Jacob and I continue to live a healthy gluten free lifestyle.

Bread & Bakery

Bagels

2023 Annual Gluten Free Awards

1st Place Winner: Canyon Bakehouse Everything Bagel

2nd Place Winner: MYBREAD Gluten Free Bakery Original Bagels

3rd Place Winner: Little Northern Bakehouse Gluten Free Everything Bagels

Runner Up:

Trader Joe's Everything Bagel

Other Great Products:

O'Doughs Everything Bagels

Schar Plain Bagels

Bread

2023 Annual Gluten Free Awards

1st Place Winner: Canyon Bakehouse Mountain White

2nd Place Winner: Canyon Bakehouse Hawaiian Sweet Bread

3rd Place Winner: Schar Artisan Baker White

Runner Up:

ALDI-exclusive liveGfree White Wide Pan Bread

Other Great Products:

MYBREAD Gluten Free Bakery Original Baguettes

ALDI-exclusive liveGfree Whole Grain Wide Pan Bread

BFree Foods Stone Baked Pita Bread

BFree Foods Stone Baked Naan Bread

BFree Foods Stone Baked Wholegrain Pita

DID YOU KNOW?

CELIAC DISEASE CASES DOUBLE EVERY 15 YEARS IN THE UNITED STATES

Quoted from:
17th International Celiac Disease
Symposium in New Delhi, India

Breadcrumbs

2023 Annual Gluten Free Awards

1st Place Winner: Aleia's Best. Taste. Ever. Italian Bread-crumbs

2nd Place Winner: Aleia's Best. Taste. Ever. Panko

3rd Place Winner: Aleia's Best. Taste. Ever. Coat & Crunch Extra Crispy

Runner Up:

4C Gluten Free Seasoned Breadcrumbs

Other Great Products:

Gillian's Italian GF Breadcrumbs

Schar Bread Crumbs

Buns

2023 Annual Gluten Free Awards

1st Place Winner: Canyon Bakehouse Stay Fresh Burger Buns

2nd Place Winner: BFree Foods Burger Buns

3rd Place Winner: Little Northern Bakehouse Millet and Chia Gluten Free Hamburger Bun

Runner Up:

Schar Hamburger Buns

Other Great Buns:

Trader Joe's Gluten Free Hamburger Buns

CELIAC SURVEY

We polled over 1000 people with celiac disease with the intent to make you feel not so alone.

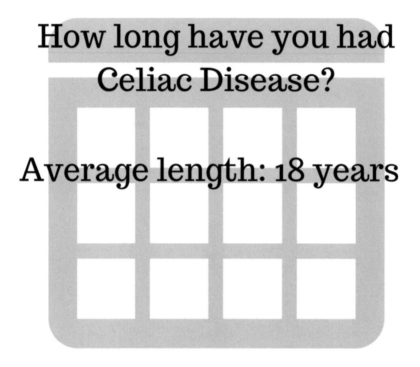

How long have you had Celiac Disease?

Average length: 18 years

Presented by The 2023 Gluten Free Buyers Guide

YOU'RE NOT ALONE

Cookies

2023 Annual Gluten Free Awards

1st Place Winner: Schär Chocolate Honeygrams

2nd Place Winner: ALDI-exclusive Benton's Chocolatey Coconut Macaroons

3rd Place Winner: Mary's Gone Kookies Chocolate

Runner Up:

Nabisco Gluten Free Oreos

Other Great Products:

ALDI-exclusive Benton's Coconut Macaroons

Mary's Gone Kookies Cinnamon

Mary's Gone Kookies Honey

Tate's Bake Shop Gluten Free Chocolate Chip Cookies

You know you are gluten free

THE GUIDED BUYER.COM

When your bun costs more than the burger

Pizza Crust

2023 Annual Gluten Free Awards

1st Place Winner: gf Jules Gluten Free Pizza Crust Mix

2nd Place Winner: CAULIPOWER Cauliflower Pizza Crust

3rd Place Winner: MYBREAD Gluten Free Bakery Original Pizza Crusts

Runner Up:

BFree Foods Stone Baked Pizza Crust

Other Great Products:

Cappello's Naked Pizza Crust

Against The Grain Gourmet Pizza Shell

DID YOU KNOW?

1:2 IN THE UNITED STATES WILL TRY A GLUTEN-FREE DIET THIS YEAR

Quoted from:
17th International Celiac Disease
Symposium in New Delhi, India

Rolls

2023 Annual Gluten Free Awards

1st Place Winner: Canyon Bakehouse Brioche-Style Sweet Rolls

2nd Place Winner: Against the Grain Gourmet Rolls

3rd Place Winner: MYBREAD Gluten Free Bakery Original Dinner Rolls

Runner Up:

Schar Ciabatta Rolls

Other Great Products:

BFree Foods Panini Rolls

BFree Foods White Demi Baguettes

Tortilla

2023 Annual Gluten Free Awards

1st Place Winner: Mission Soft Corn Tortilla

2nd Place Winner: Mission Gluten Free Tortillas

3rd Place Winner: Siete Almond Flour Tortillas

Runner Up:

Tia Lupita Grain Free Tortillas

Other Great Products:

La Tortilla Factory Gluten Free Tortillas, Cassava Flour

Wrap

2023 Annual Gluten Free Awards

1st Place Winner: Mission Gluten Free Original Tortilla Wraps

2nd Place Winner: BFree Foods Stone Baked Pita Bread

3rd Place Winner: MYBREAD Gluten Free Bakery Original Flatbread Pitas

Runner Up:

BFree Foods Sweet Potato Wrap

Other Great Products:

BFree Foods Avocado Wrap

CELIAC SURVEY

We polled over 1000 people with celiac disease with the intent to make you feel not so alone.

Have you helped anyone get diagnosed with Celiac Disease?

56% Yes

44% No

Presented by The 2023 Gluten Free Buyers Guide

YOU'RE NOT ALONE

Breakfast

Breakfast On-The-Go

2023 Annual Gluten Free Awards

1st Place Winner: Bob's Red Mill Gluten Free Brown Sugar Maple Oatmeal Cup

2nd Place Winner: CAULIPOWER Broccoli Cheddar Scramble

3rd Place Winner: Feel Good Foods Potato, Egg & Cheese Pockets

Runner Up:

Real Good Foods Breakfast Sandwich Sausage, Egg & Cheese

Other Great Products:

Goodie Girl Cinnamon Brown Sugar Breakfast Biscuits

Glutino English Muffins

Cold Cereals

2023 Annual Gluten Free Awards

1st Place Winner: General Mills Cinnamon Chex

2nd Place Winner: Magic Spoon – Frosted

3rd Place Winner: Three Wishes Cocoa

Runner Up:

General Mills Peanut Butter Chex

Other Great Products:

Nature's Path Corn Flakes

CELIAC SURVEY

We polled over 1000 people with celiac disease with the intent to make you feel not so alone.

Have you ever had a nightmare about eating something with gluten?

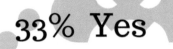

33% Yes

67% No

Presented by The 2023 Gluten Free Buyers Guide

YOU'RE NOT ALONE

Donuts

2023 Annual Gluten Free Awards

1st Place Winner: Katz Gluten Free Glazed Donuts

2nd Place Winner: ALDI-exclusive liveGfree Gluten Free Glazed Donuts

3rd Place Winner: Katz Gluten Free Powdered Donuts

Runner Up:

Katz Gluten Free Custard Filled Donuts

Other Great Products:

ALDI-exclusive liveGfree Gluten Free Chocolate Donuts

You know you are gluten free

When you blow your
paycheck at the grocery store

Frozen Pancake & Waffle Brands

2023 Annual Gluten Free Awards

1st Place Winner: Vanilla Viking Waffles

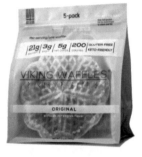

2nd Place Winner: Van's Gluten Free Frozen Waffles

3rd Place Winner:

Lopaus Point Wild Blueberry Waffles

Runner Up:

Birch Benders Paleo Toaster Waffles

Other Great Products:

Nature's Path Dark Chocolate Chip Waffles, Gluten Free Frozen Waffles

DID YOU KNOW?

GLUTEN CAN'T BE DIGESTED BY HUMAN BODY (LONG CHAIN AMINO ACID)

Quoted from:
17th International Celiac Disease
Symposium in New Delhi, India

Pancake and Waffle Mixes

2023 Annual Gluten Free Awards

1st Place Winner: gf Jules Pancake & Waffle Mix

2nd Place Winner: Better Batter Pancake and Biscuit Mix

3rd Place Winner: King Arthur Gluten Free Pancake Mix

Runner Up:

Betty Crocker Gluten Free Bisquick

Other Great Products:

Pamela's Baking & Pancake Mix

CELIAC SURVEY

We polled over 1000 people with celiac disease with the intent to make you feel not so alone.

Do you have anxiety when eating out on a gluten free diet?

78% Yes

22% No

Presented by The 2023 Gluten Free Buyers Guide

YOU'RE NOT ALONE

Cookies, Snacks & Candy

Candy

2023 Annual Gluten Free Awards

1st Place Winner: Justin's Dark Chocolate Peanut Butter Crispy Cups

2nd Place Winner: No Whey! Milkless Crunchy

3rd Place Winner: Schär Twin Bar

Runner Up:

Enjoy Life Ricemilk Chocolate Crunch Bars

Other Great Products:

Hershey Milk Chocolate Bar

Chips

2023 Annual Gluten Free Awards

1st Place Winner: Siete Foods Ranch Grain Free Tortilla Chips

2nd Place Winner: ALDI-exclusive Simply Nature White Cheddar Puffs

3rd Place Winner: Food Should Taste Good Sweet Potato Tortilla Chips

Runner Up:

Lay's Classic Chips

Other Great Products:

ALDI-exclusive Clancy's Veggie Chips

ALDI-exclusive Clancy's Veggie Straws

DID YOU KNOW?

30-50% OF WORLD POPULATION HAS A GENETIC PREDISPOSITION TO CELIAC DISEASE

Quoted from:
17th International Celiac Disease
Symposium in New Delhi, India

Crackers

2023 Annual Gluten Free Awards

1st Place Winner: Mary's Gone Crackers REAL Thin Sea Salt

2nd Place Winner: Schär Gluten Free Table Crackers

3rd Place Winner: Simple Mills Farmhouse Cheddar

Runner Up:

Milton's Crispy Sea Salt Baked Crackers

Other Great Products:

Blue Diamond Nut Thins

CELIAC SURVEY

We polled over 1000 people with celiac disease with the intent to make you feel not so alone.

Do you like to eat out or at home?

80% Home

20% Out

Presented by The 2023 Gluten Free Buyers Guide

YOU'RE NOT ALONE

Granola

2023 Annual Gluten Free Awards

1st Place Winner: Bear Naked Maple Cinnamon Gluten Free Granola

2nd Place Winner: ALDI-exclusive Simply Nature Gluten Free Cranberry Cashew Granola

3rd Place Winner: KIND Almond Butter Clusters

Runner Up: ALDI-exclusive Simply Nature Gluten Free Apple Almond Honey Granola

Other Great Products:

Purely Elizabeth Original

ALDI-exclusive Simply Nature Gluten Free Raisin Almond Honey Granola

Jerky

2023 Annual Gluten Free Awards

1st Place Winner: Chomps Original Beef Jerky Sticks

2nd Place Winner: Country Archer Original Beef Jerky

3rd Place Winner: Chomps Turkey Jerky Sticks

Runner Up:

Lorissa's Kitchen Korean BBQ jerky

Other Great Products:

Krave Chili Lime

Munchies

2023 Annual Gluten Free Awards

1st Place Winner: SkinnyPop Popcorn

2nd Place Winner: Mary's Gone Crackers Original

3rd Place Winner: Mary's Gone Crackers Super Seed Classic

Runner Up:

Snyder's of Hanover Gluten Free Mini Pretzels

Other Great Products:

Quinn's Peanut Butter filled Pretzel Nuggets

DID YOU KNOW?

1–100 AD: woman has celiac disease genes and damage.

In 2008, an archaeological dig in Italy revealed an 18-20-year-old woman from the first century AD, with signs of failure to thrive and malnutrition. The skeleton showed the presence of a celiac gene and damage typically seen from celiac disease.

Source:
Beyond Celiac

Popcorn

2023 Annual Gluten Free Awards

1st Place Winner: SkinnyPop Popcorn

2nd Place Winner: Angie's BOOMCHICKAPOP Sweet & Salty Kettle Corn

3rd Place Winner: ALDI-exclusive Clancy's White Cheddar Cheese Popcorn

Runner Up:

Lesser Evil "No Cheese" Cheesiness

Other Great Products:

Smartfood® White Cheddar Popcorn

Pretzels

2023 Annual Gluten Free Awards

1st Place Winner: Snyder's of Hanover Gluten Free Pretzel Sticks

2nd Place Winner: Quinn Snacks Non-GMO and Gluten Free Pretzels, Classic Sea Salt

3rd Place Winner: Savor Street Grain Free Pretzel Twists - Gluten Free - Paleo Friendly

Runner Up:

Glutino Pretzel Twists

Other Great Products:

FitJoy Grain Free Pretzels, Gluten Free

Snack Bars

2023 Annual Gluten Free Awards

1st Place Winner: Annie's Organic Gluten Free Double Chocolate Chip Granola Bars

2nd Place Winner: BeBOLD Bars Chocolate Chip Almond Butter

3rd Place Winner: KIND Caramel, Almond, & Sea Salt

Runner Up:

KIND Peanut Butter Dark Chocolate

Other Great Products:

Nature's Bakery Blueberry Gluten Free Fig Bars

DID YOU KNOW?

1952: Medical team publishes their findings about wheat and rye flour and celiac disease.

The English medical team shared results of studies showing how celiac disease patients improved when wheat and rye flour was removed from their diets. Gluten, the protein found in wheat, barley and rye, was later pinpointed as the exact trigger for celiac disease.

Source:
Beyond Celiac

Dessert

Ice Cream Cones

2023 Annual Gluten Free Awards

1st Place Winner: Joy Gluten-Free Sugar Ice Cream Cones

2nd Place Winner: Joy Gluten-Free Ice Cream Cones Cake Cups

3rd Place Winner: Sprouts Coconut Cones

Runner Up: Let's Do Gluten Free Ice Cream Cones

Other Great Products:

Let's Do Gluten Sugar Ice Cream Cones

CELIAC SURVEY

We polled over 1000 people with celiac disease with the intent to make you feel not so alone.

Opinion: How long will it take before they find a cure for Celiac Disease?

Average: 36 More Years

Presented by The 2023 Gluten Free Buyers Guide

YOU'RE NOT ALONE

Pie Crust

2023 Annual Gluten Free Awards

1st Place Winner: Wholly Wholesome Gluten Free Pie Crusts

2nd Place Winner: King Arthur Gluten-Free Pie Crust

3rd Place Winner: Trader Joes Gluten Free Pie Crust (frozen)

Runner Up:

Midel Graham Cracker Crust

Other Great Products:

The Maine Pie Co. Gluten Free Pie Shells

Ready Made Desserts

2023 Annual Gluten Free Awards

1st Place Winner: Wholly Gluten Free 5 Pack Fudge Brownies

2nd Place Winner: Ethel's Baking Company Pecan Dandy

3rd Place Winner: Katz Gluten Free Personal Size Cherry Pie

Runner Up:

Daiya Gluten Free Cheesecake

Other Great Products:

FatBoy® Gluten-Free Ice Cream Cone

Celiac Survey

We polled over 1000 people with celiac disease with the intent to make you feel not so alone.

Is it harder to date others when you are on a gluten free diet?

44% No
56% Yes

Presented by The 2023 Gluten Free Buyers Guide

YOU'RE NOT ALONE

Beverages

Beer

2023 Annual Gluten Free Awards

1st Place Winner: Glutenberg

2nd Place Winner: Bards

3rd Place Winner: Ground Breaker Brewing

Runner Up:

Ghostfish Brewing

Other Great Beers:

Holidaily Brewing

Alt Brew

DID YOU KNOW?

1887: Dr. Samuel Gee writes the first modern medical description of celiac disease and hypothesizes it can be treated through diet.

He says people with "celiac affection" can be cured by diet. Gee first presented the modern definition of celiac disease at a lecture for Sick Children in London. However, during his lifetime he was never able to pinpoint which food triggered the disease.

Source:
Beyond Celiac

Hard Seltzer

2023 Annual Gluten Free Awards

1st Place Winner: Truly Lemonade Seltzer

2nd Place Winner: ALDI-exclusive Vista Bay Hard Seltzer Variety Pack

3rd Place Winner: White Claw

You know you are gluten free

When you blame your hangover on gluten

Dry Mixes

Bread Mixes

2023 Annual Gluten Free Awards

1st Place Winner: gfJules Bread Mix

2nd Place Winner: Pamela's Products Amazing Gluten-free Bread Mix

3rd Place Winner: King Arthur Gluten-Free Bread and Pizza Mix

Runner Up:

Simple Mills Gluten Free Artisan Bread Mix

Other Great Products:

Red Lobster Gluten Free Cheddar Bay Biscuit Mix

CELIAC SURVEY

We polled over 1000 people with celiac disease
with the intent to make you feel not so alone.

Have you
ever knowingly cheated
on your gluten free diet?

28% Yes

72% No

Presented by The 2023 Gluten Free Buyers Guide

YOU'RE NOT ALONE

Brownie Mixes

2023 Annual Gluten Free Awards

1st Place Winner: Better Batter Fudge Brownie Mix

2nd Place Winner: ALDI-exclusive liveGfree Gluten Free Brownie Baking Mix

3rd Place Winner: King Arthur Gluten Free Brownie Mix

Runner Up:

Krusteaz Gluten Free Double Chocolate Brownie Mix

Other Great Products:

Betty Crocker Gluten Free Brownie Mix

You know you are gluten free

THE GUIDED BUYER.COM

When you have nightmares about eating regular food

Cake Mixes

2023 Annual Gluten Free Awards

1st Place Winner: gfJules Gluten Free Cake Mix

2nd Place Winner: Better Batter Chocolate Cake Mix

3rd Place Winner: ALDI-exclusive liveGfree Gluten Free Yellow Cake Baking Mix

Runner Up: Better Batter Yellow Cake Mix

Other Great Products:

King Arthur Flour Gluten Free Chocolate Cake Mix

CELIAC SURVEY

We polled over 1000 people with celiac disease with the intent to make you feel not so alone.

After consuming gluten, do you have symptoms?

89% Yes Symptoms

11% No Symptoms

Presented by The 2023 Gluten Free Buyers Guide

YOU'RE NOT ALONE

Cookie Mixes

2023 Annual Gluten Free Awards

1st Place Winner: gfJules Cookie Mix

2nd Place Winner: 365 by Whole Foods Market, Chocolate Chip Gluten Free Cookie Mix

3rd Place Winner: Betty Crocker Gluten Free Chocolate Chip Cookie Mix

Runner Up:

Bob's Red Mill: Gluten Free Chocolate Chip Cookie Mix

Other Great Products:

Pillsbury™ Gluten Free Chocolate Chip Cookie Mix

CELIAC SURVEY

We polled over 1000 people with celiac disease with the intent to make you feel not so alone.

Do you have other family with Celiac Disease?

48% Yes

52% No

Presented by The 2023 Gluten Free Buyers Guide

YOU'RE NOT ALONE

Cornbread Mixes

2023 Annual Gluten Free Awards

1st Place Winner: gfJules Cornbread Mix

2nd Place Winner: Krusteaz Gluten Free Honey Cornbread Mix

3rd Place Winner: Cup4Cup Gluten Free Cornbread Mix

Runner Up: Bob's Red Mill Cornbread Mix

Other Great Products:

ALDI-exclusive liveGfree Gluten Free Cornbread Mix

Flours

2023 Annual Gluten Free Awards

1st Place Winner: gfJules All Purpose Gluten Free Flour

2nd Place Winner: Better Batter Original Blend

3rd Place Winner: Better Batter Artisan Blend

Runner Up:

Bob's Red Mill Gluten Free 1-to-1 Baking Flour

Other Great Products:

King Arthur Measure for Measure Gluten Free Flour

DID YOU KNOW?

1970s-1990s: Celiac disease is recognized as an autoimmune disease and genes are pinpointed.

By the early 1990s, celiac disease is accepted as an autoimmune disease with a specific gene (either HLA-DQ2 or HLA-DQ8). While in 1997, The role of the antigen tissue transglutaminase (TtG) in celiac disease is discovered.

Source:
Beyond Celiac

Muffin Mixes

2023 Annual Gluten Free Awards

1st Place Winner: gf Jules Muffin Mix

2nd Place Winner: King Arthur Gluten Free Muffin Mix

3rd Place Winner: Krusteaz Gluten Free Blueberry Muffin Mix

Runner Up:

Highkey Healthy Gluten Free Blueberry Muffin

Other Great Products:

Lakanto Gluten Free Banana Nut Muffin and Bread Mix

Frozen Foods

Frozen Meals

2023 Annual Gluten Free Awards

1st Place Winner: Primal Kitchen Chicken Pesto Bowl

2nd Place Winner: ALDI-exclusive Whole & Simple Southwest Chicken Quinoa Bowl

3rd Place Winner: Amy's Gluten Free Rice Mac & Cheese

Runner Up:

ALDI-exclusive Whole & Simple Mediterranean Chicken Quinoa Bowl

Other Great Products:

Feel Good Foods Potstickers

CELIAC SURVEY

We polled over 1000 people with celiac disease
with the intent to make you feel not so alone.

Do you pack gluten free food in your baggage when traveling?

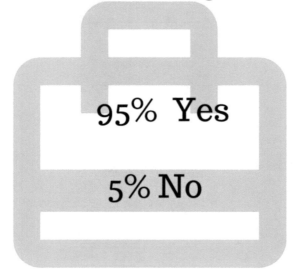

95% Yes

5% No

Presented by The 2023 Gluten Free Buyers Guide

YOU'RE NOT ALONE

Frozen Pizza Brands

2023 Annual Gluten Free Awards

1st Place Winner: Freschetta Gluten Free Pepperoni Pizza

2nd Place Winner: DiGiorno Gluten Free Pepperoni Frozen Pizza

3rd Place Winner: CAULIPOWER Cauliflower Crust Pizza Margherita

Runner Up:

Against the Grain Pesto Pizza

Other Great Products:

Sabatasso's Gluten Free Four Cheese Pizza

CELIAC SURVEY

We polled over 1000 people with celiac disease with the intent to make you feel not so alone.

At work, are you the only one with Celiac Disease?

77% Yes

Presented by The 2023 Gluten Free Buyers Guide

YOU'RE NOT ALONE

Health & Beauty

Cosmetic Brands

2023 Annual Gluten Free Awards

1st Place Winner: Red Apple Lipstick

2nd Place Winner: Arbonne

3rd Place Winner: Honeybee Gardens

Runner Up:
Ilia Beauty

ILIA

Other Great Products:
Gabriel Cosmetics

GABRIEL

Magazine & Books

Books

2023 Annual Gluten Free Awards

1st Place Winner: The First Year: Celiac Disease and Living Gluten-Free: An Essential Guide for the Newly Diagnosed: Jules Shepard

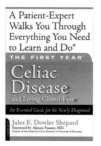

2nd Place Winner: Dear Gluten, It's Not Me, It's You: How to Survive Without Gluten and Restore Your Health from Celiac Disease or Gluten Sensitivity by Jenny Levine Finke and Dr. Tom O'Bryan

3rd Place Winner: Gluten Freedom: The Nation's Leading Expert Offers the Essential Guide to a Healthy, Gluten-Free Lifestyle by Alessio Fasano (Author), Susie Flaherty (Contributor)

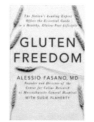

Runner Up:

Gluten Is My Bitch: Rants, Recipes, and Ridiculousness for the Gluten-Free

Other Great Books:

Living Gluten-Free For Dummies

CELIAC SURVEY

We polled over 1000 people with celiac disease with the intent to make you feel not so alone.

Do you drink gluten removed beer or stick to gluten free beers?

80% Gluten Free Only

12% Both

8% Gluten Removed

Presented by The 2023 Gluten Free Buyers Guide

YOU'RE NOT ALONE

Children's Books

2023 Annual Gluten Free Awards

1st Place Winner: Everyone's Got Something: My First Year with Celiac Disease by Hallie Rose Katzman, Rayna Mae Katzman

2nd Place Winner: Eat Like a Dinosaur: Recipe & Guidebook for Gluten-free Kids by Paleo Parents and Elana Amsterdam

3rd Place Winner: My Perfect Cupcake: A Recipe for Thriving with Food Allergies (The Fearless Food Allergy Friends) by Rebecca Greene and Rebecca Sinclair

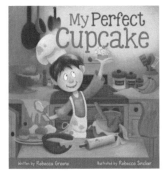

Runner Up:

Gluten Free is Part of Me by Laurie Oestreich

Other Great Books:

I'm a Gluten-Sniffing Service Dog by Michal Babay (Author), Ela Smietanka (Illustrator)

DID YOU KNOW?

People recently diagnosed with celiac disease are commonly deficient in fiber, iron, calcium, magnesium, zinc, folate, niacin, riboflavin, vitamin B12, and vitamin D.

Source:
Celiac Disease Foundation

Cookbooks

2023 Annual Gluten Free Awards

1st Place Winner: Nearly Normal Cooking For Gluten-Free Eating: A Fresh Approach to Cooking and Living Without Wheat or Gluten by Jules E. D. Shepard and Alessio Fasano

2nd Place Winner: How to Make Anything Gluten-Free: Over 100 recipes for everything from home comforts to fakeaways, cakes to dessert, brunch to bread! by Becky Excell

3rd Place Winner: Cook Once, Eat All Week: 26 Weeks of Gluten-Free, Affordable Meal Prep to Preserve Your Time & Sanity by Cassy Joy Garcia

Runner Up: Flavcity's 5 Ingredient Meals: 50 Easy & Tasty Recipes Using the Best Ingredients from the Grocery Store (Heart Healthy Budget Cooking) by Bobby Parrish & Dessi Parrish

Other Great Cookbooks:

The Defined Dish: Whole30 Endorsed, Healthy and Wholesome Weeknight Recipes Hardcover by Alex Snodgrass

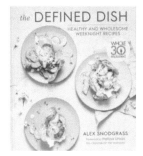

Gluten-Free on a Shoestring: 125 Easy Recipes for Eating Well on the Cheap by Nicole Hunn

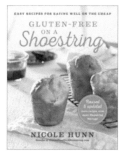

You know you are gluten free

THE GUIDED BUYER.COM

When you pack more food than clothes

Magazines

2023 Annual Gluten Free Awards

1st Place Winner: Simply Gluten Free

2nd Place Winner: GFF Magazine

3rd Place Winner: Allergic Living

CELIAC SURVEY

We polled over 1000 people with celiac disease with the intent to make you feel not so alone.

Do you have a dedicated gluten free toaster in your kitchen?

71% Yes

29% No

Presented by The 2023 Gluten Free Buyers Guide

YOU'RE NOT ALONE

Media

Blogs & Websites

2023 Annual Gluten Free Awards

1st Place Winner: GFJules.com

2nd Place Winner: GlutenFreeFollowMe.com

3rd Place Winner: WhatTheForkFoodBlog.com

Runner Up:

GlutenFreeOnAShoestring.com

Other Great Blogs & Websites:

GlutenFreeGlobetrotter.com

MamaKnowsGlutenFree.com

Mobile Apps

2023 Annual Gluten Free Awards

1ˢᵗ Place Winner: Find Me Gluten Free

2ⁿᵈ Place Winner: The Gluten Free Scanner

3ʳᵈ Place Winner: Gluten Dude Mobile App

Runner Up: Spokin

Other Great Apps:

Spoonful

Nonprofits

2023 Annual Gluten Free Awards

1st Place Winner: Celiac Disease Foundation (CDF)

2nd Place Winner: Gluten Intolerance Group of North America (GIG)

3rd Place Winner: Beyond Celiac

Runner Up: National Celiac Organization

Online Resources

2023 Annual Gluten Free Awards

1st Place Winner: Celiac.org

2nd Place Winner: GlutenFreeWatchDog.org

3rd Place Winner: Beyondceliac.org

Runner Up: Glutenfreefollowme.com

Other Great Resources:

gfJules.com

VOTED #1 GLUTEN FREE FLOUR & MIXES

IN 2020 FOR THE 4TH TIME!

CELIAC SURVEY

We polled over 1000 people with celiac disease
with the intent to make you feel not so alone.

Does your family support your gluten free lifestyle?

96% Yes

4% No

Presented by The 2023 Gluten Free Buyers Guide

YOU'RE NOT ALONE

Podcasts

2023 Annual Gluten Free Awards

1st Place Winner: Gluten Free You & Me

2nd Place Winner: Gluten Free New with Andrea Tucker

3rd Place Winner: Celiac Straight Talk by Beyond Celiac

Runner Up:

The Celiac Project Podcast

Other Great Podcasts:

Celiac & Gluten Free Living with Deb

DID YOU KNOW?

Celiac disease can develop at any age after people start eating foods or medications that contain gluten.

Source:
Celiac Disease Foundation

Other

Comfort Foods

2023 Annual Gluten Free Awards

1st Place Winner: Amy's Gluten Free Rice Mac & Cheese

2nd Place Winner: MYBREAD Gluten Free Bakery Original Soft Breadsticks

3rd Place Winner: Feel Good Foods Three Cheese Mac & Cheese Bites

Runner Up:

Feel Good Foods Mozzarella Sticks

Other Great Products:

Kraft Gluten Free Mac and Cheese

New Products

2023 Annual Gluten Free Awards

1st Place Winner: Canyon Bakehouse Stay Fresh Brioche-Style Sweet Rolls

2nd Place Winner: San-J Tamari Splash Umami

3rd Place Winner: Mary's Gone Kookies Cinnamon

Runner Up:

Gluten-Free Buffalo Chicken Egg Rolls

Other Great Products:

Snow Days Gluten Free Pizza Bites

CELIAC SURVEY

We polled over 1000 people with celiac disease
with the intent to make you feel not so alone.

Have you gained or lost weight on a gluten free diet?

65% Gained weight

35% Lost weight

Presented by The 2023 Gluten Free Buyers Guide

YOU'RE NOT ALONE

Pasta, Sides, Soup & Sauces

Macaroni and Cheese

2023 Annual Gluten Free Awards

1st Place Winner: Kraft Gluten Free Macaroni & Cheese

2nd Place Winner: ALDI-exclusive liveGfree Gluten Free Deluxe Macaroni & Cheese

3rd Place Winner: Amy's Gluten Free Macaroni & Cheese

Runner Up:
Annie's Gluten Free Rice Shell Pasta with Creamy White Cheddar

Other Great Products:

Trader Joe's Frozen Gluten Free Mac & Cheese

Pastas

2023 Annual Gluten Free Awards

1st Place Winner: Barilla Spaghetti

2nd Place Winner: Already Spaghetti Ready to Eat Spaghetti Squash

3rd Place Winner: CAULIPOWER Linguine Cauliflower Pasta

Runner Up:

Jovial Tagliatelle

Other Great Products:

Tinkyada Brown Rice Spirals

Condiments

2023 Annual Gluten Free Awards

1st Place Winner: San-J Hoisin Sauce

2nd Place Winner: Mike's Hot Honey

3rd Place Winner: Noble Made by The New Primal Tomato Ketchup

Runner Up:

San-J Organic Tamari Soy Sauce

Other Great Products:

Chosen Foods Avocado Mayo

Dips and Spreads

2023 Annual Gluten Free Awards

1st Place Winner: ALDI-exclusive Park Street Deli Classic Guacamole Cups

2nd Place Winner: Skinnygirl Sugar Free Preserves, Apricot Mimosa

3rd Place Winner: ALDI-exclusive Park Street Deli Spicy Guacamole Cups

Runner Up:

Chipotle Bitchin' Sauce

Other Great Products:

Chick-fil-A Sauce

Dressing

2023 Annual Gluten Free Awards

1st Place Winner: Yo Mama's Foods American Ranch

2nd Place Winner: Wu Japanese Gluten Free Ginger Dressing

3rd Place Winner: Hidden Valley Ranch

Runner Up:

Ken's Steak House Ranch

Other Great Products:

Brianna's Blush Wine Vinaigrette

CELIAC SURVEY

We polled over 1000 people with celiac disease with the intent to make you feel not so alone.

Do you think the celebrity / Hollywood gluten free trend helped or hurt those with Celiac Disease?

54% Hurt

46% Helped

Presented by The 2023 Gluten Free Buyers Guide

YOU'RE NOT ALONE

Sauces

2023 Annual Gluten Free Awards

1st Place Winner: San-J Organic Gluten Free Tamari Soy Sauce

2nd Place Winner: Kevin's Natural Foods Teriyaki Sauce - Keto, Gluten Free & Paleo Simmer Sauce

3rd Place Winner: Kikkoman Gluten Free Teriyaki

Runner Up:

Frontera Foods Green Enchilada Sauce

Other Great Products:

Trader Joe's Organic Coconut Aminos

CELIAC SURVEY

We polled over 1000 people with celiac disease with the intent to make you feel not so alone.

Have people made fun of the gluten free diet in front of you?

58% Yes

Presented by The 2023 Gluten Free Buyers Guide

YOU'RE NOT ALONE

Soup

2023 Annual Gluten Free Awards

1st Place Winner: Progresso New England Clam Chowder

2nd Place Winner: Progresso Chicken Rice with Vegetables

3rd Place Winner: Thai Kitchen Instant Rice Noodle Soup - Gluten Free Ramen

Runner Up:

Amy's Split Pea

Other Great Products:

Snapdragon Mushroom Gluten Free Pho Bowls

CELIAC SURVEY

We polled over 1000 people with celiac disease with the intent to make you feel not so alone.

Do you attend any celiac support group meetings?

30% Yes

70% No

Presented by The 2023 Gluten Free Buyers Guide

YOU'RE NOT ALONE

Stuffing

2023 Annual Gluten Free Awards

1st Place Winner: Aleia's Best. Taste. Ever. Savory Stuffing

2nd Place Winner: Aleia's Best. Taste. Ever. Plain Stuffing

3rd Place Winner: Olivia's Croutons - Rosemary & Sage Stuffing

Runner Up:

Trader Joes Gluten Free Stuffing Mix (Seasonal)

Other Great Products:

Aldi liveGfree Gluten Free Chicken Stuffing Mix (Seasonal)

Personalities

Best Gluten Free Personality

2023 Annual Gluten Free Awards

1st Place Winner: Jules Shepard

2nd Place Winner: Christina Kantzavelos

3rd Place Winner: Patrick Auger

Runner Up: Jen Bigler

Other great gluten free people:

Gluten Dude

Erica Dermer

Andrea Tucker

Erin Smith

Phil Hates Gluten

Mike Frolichstein

Jackie Aanonsen McEwan

Jackie McEwan

How long have you been gluten free?

8+ years

Do you have any other dietary restrictions?

Just gluten

What has been your biggest challenge thus far?

My biggest challenge was when I found out that I had to follow a gluten-free diet. I was completely overwhelmed. I did not even know what gluten was! I had to figure out what foods I could eat, what foods I had to avoid, and the nuances in between. I wished I had a go-to guide to tell me all I needed to know about following a gluten-free diet. This manual did not yet exist, so I did a ton of research and learned how to maneuver being gluten-free at restaurants and in my own kitchen.

In March 2014, I started to post about some of the gluten-free foods I was eating on Instagram. Surprisingly to me, my posts were met with great reception. People I had never met were asking me for more tips on gluten-free friendly eateries, products, and recipes, and I was more than happy to continue to make these discoveries. I was getting so many questions that I knew I needed to put all this information in one place rather than just Instagram.

In September 2014, I taught myself how to make a website, and I launched glutenfreefollowme.com! I wish I had something like Gluten Free Follow Me to guide me through my new gluten-free diet eight years ago, but I am glad I can be a guide for others now! At the time, going gluten-free seemed like the worst thing ever. However, I am grateful for it now. Knowledge is power, and I am healthier because of it. Going gluten-free led me to start Gluten Free Follow Me. If I had not become gluten-free, I would probably still be working in finance in New York City. My quest to find gluten-free foods developed into a full-time passion, and I could not be happier with how it all turned out!

Where is your favorite place to eat?

I have many favorites! A few of my faves are: Posh Pop Bakeshop in NYC, Vibe Organic Kitchen in Newport Beach, and Petunia's Pies & Pastries in Portland. Many more on glutenfreefollowme.com/restaurants :)

Do you have any gluten related pet peeves?

When someone says that they could never give up gluten. When you have to, yes you can! And honestly, it's not that hard, especially nowadays. There are so many amazing options.

Do you have a gluten horror story?

Back when I was working in NYC, I went out to lunch at a restaurant that is now closed. I told the hostess, manager, and waitress that I was gluten-free. They went through the menu with me and told me which options were safe for me to eat. I ended up ordering the nachos as an appetizer. I had just taken my first bite of the nachos when the manager ran over to tell me that the nachos were not actually gluten-free. The chips had cross contamination in the fryer. I couldn't believe it! It was even more frustrating because I had asked the right questions. Thankfully, something like this hasn't happened to me again.

What has been the biggest change since you became gluten free?

Every year, it becomes easier to follow a gluten-free diet! It's more straightforward to find gluten-free foods. Supermarkets and stores now have gluten-free sections, and food labeling has gotten better. Products market themselves to the gluten-free consumer. Some brands have even modified their ingredients in order to make their products gluten-free. The restaurant scene has become more sensitive to people who follow a gluten-free diet. Some restaurants have menus that indicate which items are gluten-free, and this definitely wasn't the case seven years ago. Waiters are usually well-versed in how to accommodate dietary needs, unlike a few years ago when the majority of waiters didn't even know what gluten was.

In ten years, a gluten free diet will be···

Even more widespread. I see the gluten-free world continuing down the path of increased awareness. I've eaten at 75 completely gluten-free eateries, and I expect to see even more 100% gluten-free eateries in the future. I predict that the number of people who go gluten-free will keep on multiplying. After all, gluten-free food truly tastes good now, and it's a healthier way to live.

What is the best advice you received?

Make something people want.

What is the best way for people to connect with you?

Instagram: @glutenfree.followme

Twitter: @glutenfreefm

Facebook: Gluten Free Follow Me

Blog: glutenfreefollowme.com

Phil Hates Gluten

How long have you been gluten free?

About 4 years

Do you have any other dietary restrictions?

Yup! Dairy (EOE) and Shellfish (allergy).

What has been your biggest challenge thus far?

Probably not being as spontaneous as I used to be. I was never much of a planner but I'm learning to become one so that I know I can eat something safely. For example, now instead of just carrying my phone and wallet around, I got two protein bars stuffed into my pocket at any given time.

Where is your favorite place to eat?

Bartaco is the first restaurant that comes to mind. Great guac, fun chips to crack apart, amazing plantains, unreal tacos, and my favorite margaritas. Now my mouth is watering, I might have to go tonight...

Do you have any gluten related pet peeves?

Not necessarily a pet peeve, but since becoming gluten free I've noticed just how much food has gluten in it. Like especially, snacks, breakfast items, fast food, etc. It's pretty crazy and sometimes frustrating to find something to eat.

Do you have a gluten horror story?

While I was sort've figuring my food triggers out, I was advised to do a "gluten challenge" to make sure I wasn't allergic to it. So I ate 3 pieces of regular bread after not having gluten for a year or so. Turns out that was bad planning by me, because I was meeting my girlfriend's mom for the first time the next day. Let's just say the floodgates opened in all the wrong ways at all the wrong times.

What has been the biggest change since you became gluten free?

Probably creating an entire online presence about it haha. But besides that, I think I've become more aware and empathetic to others with food allergies. I didn't think about it much before I was gluten free, but now when I hear someone has to eat a certain way I go out of my way to accommodate them because I know how hard it can be.

In ten years, a gluten free diet will be···

easier to do, hopefully. I live in Boston and it's relatively convenient to eat gluten free because most grocery stores and a lot of restaurants have safe options. But, it can always be better and I know other areas aren't so fortunate in that regard. Like, how dope would it be if McDonalds had gluten free buns in the US? Or Burger King had gluten free nuggets? Or more restaurants had dedicated fryers? The experience of eating out could be improved a lot for those with food restrictions, and I truly hope that it will.

What is the best advice you received?

A classic, that my mom always says, "everything happens for a reason."

What is the best way for people to connect with you?

You can find me at @philhatesgluten on Instagram, Tiktok and Youtube!

CELIAC SURVEY

We polled over 1000 people with celiac disease
with the intent to make you feel not so alone.

Do you feel alone living the gluten free lifestyle?

58% Yes

Presented by The 2023 Gluten Free Buyers Guide

YOU'RE NOT ALONE

Jules Shepard

How long have you been gluten free?

21 years!

Do you have any other dietary restrictions?

No dairy, mostly vegan and I don't do any meat.

What has been your biggest challenge thus far?

Personally, my challenge has just been if I want to eat out. I can really make anything I want for myself and my family at home, so for travel or socializing with friends at a restaurant, it can be a bit challenging, awkward and sometimes very stressful to put my trust in a restaurant instead.

Where is your favorite place to eat?

Haha ... speaking of trusting someone else! My favorite place to eat besides home (!) is no longer open. It was one of the places I looked forward to visiting when I traveled out west for gluten-free shows or to see friends, and I learned that due to the pandemic, it closed its doors. I was so sad to learn of its demise, as well as that of so many other dedicated gluten free restaurants around the country. I truly hope that we'll see a return of dedicated GF restaurants again one day once the country recovers.

Do you have any gluten related pet peeves?

Doesn't everyone?!

It still annoys me when people think that gluten is a fad or that being gluten free is some kind of choice for us. It also annoys me that there are so many food companies out there who still make bad gluten free food! It's like they don't eat their own products!! Cheap ingredients made bad food -- it's a pretty simple concept. But the end result is that gluten free food still has a bad name because of it. Gluten free food can be super delicious and people need to know that, but they have to be exposed to the right ingredients and products, so there's still a lot of work to be done.

Do you have a gluten horror story?

How many do you want? I already told you I've been gluten free for 21 years, so that's a lot of time for horror stories! I have plenty to have accumulated during that time, but also before I was diagnosed and during the 10 years I was still eating gluten before I was diagnosed and was so sick. Gluten and I really don't get along very well at all! Pretty much anyone reading this can think on their own horror stories and I've been right there with you. If you want some more specifics, I outline several in my book, The First Year: Celiac Disease and Living Gluten Free.

What has been the biggest change since you became gluten free?

People in the general population actually have heard of gluten and celiac disease! When I was diagnosed, no one (including myself) had even heard of gluten. So there have been many, many changes. There are products on the market that are made FOR people eating gluten free, products are labeled and certified gluten free, there are gluten free menus, there are blood tests for celiac disease, there is a genetic test for celiac disease ... so many changes!

In ten years, a gluten free diet will be···

Completely mainstream.

What is the best advice you received?

I didn't. There was no one to give me advice when I was told I had to go gluten free. Literally, my doctor told me I had celiac disease and couldn't eat gluten, and then he said he thought it was in bread, but wasn't sure what it was. There were no nutritionists at the time to help me, no internet resources, no books to speak of ... it was a real wasteland of information. I ate Rice Krispies cereal until I figured out for myself that malt flavoring contained barley which also contained gluten. Then I ate Peppermint Patties because I thought they didn't have any gluten in them. And rice. I ate lots of rice. It was a dark time for me! (Don't worry, I finally figured it out!)

What is the best way for people to connect with you?

@gfJules on FB, IG & Pinterest and @THEgfJules on Twitter or through my blog gfJules.com.

DID YOU KNOW?

Many people with celiac disease are asymptomatic, meaning they don't experience any external symptoms at all. However, everyone with celiac disease is still at risk for long-term complications.

Source:
Celiac Disease Foundation

CELIAC SURVEY

We polled over 1000 people with celiac disease
with the intent to make you feel not so alone.

Do you eat something before you go out to eat?

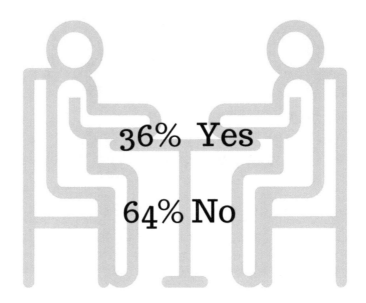

36% Yes

64% No

Presented by The 2023 Gluten Free Buyers Guide

YOU'RE NOT ALONE

Erica Dermer

How long have you been gluten free?

10-ish years! There were a few years of on and off diagnoses while I was waiting on a celiac disease true diagnosis!

Do you have any other dietary restrictions?

I can't eat beef - haven't had it in 12 or so years. I've cut out dairy for about 5-6 years, and eggs on and off for years. I now eat baked eggs (like eggs in bread).

What has been your biggest challenge thus far?

Fighting the misinformation of the internet! Unfortunately, too many still view gluten free as a "diet to try" when in reality it's a medical diet that should be given by a medical professional after a celiac disease screening.

Where is your favorite place to eat?

We're so lucky to have so many great dedicated gluten-free restaurants and bakeries here in Phoenix, and gluten-free friendly restaurants. I don't have a favorite - I just love to eat!

Do you have any gluten related pet peeves?

Brands that don't have easily accessible information on their website or social media about how their product is made and how/where they source their ingredients.

Do you have a gluten horror story?

Most of the "horror stories" revolve around front of the house servers or managers that don't understand the seriousness of making a restaurant item safe for those with celiac, after claiming it is "gluten free."

What has been the biggest change since you became gluten free?

We are so lucky - in 2020 we have so many great gluten-free products out there. Seriously, name a product and we have a gluten-free replacement out there. We've grown so much!

In ten years, a gluten free diet will be···

Hopefully better understood as a medically-necessary diet.

What is the best advice you received?

It will get easier, it just takes time.

What is the best way for people to connect with you?

Hit me up on social media or email! I love to chat about celiac disease!

Jennifer Bigler

How long have you been gluten free?

11 years this month!

Do you have any other dietary restrictions?

I am lactose intolerant and I can't have cassava.

What has been your biggest challenge thus far?

My entire family has different allergies. Trying to cook for all of us and live on a budget is the constant challenge.

Where is your favorite place to eat?

Bamboo Sushi, it's so good and celiac friendly!

Do you have any gluten related pet peeves?
I hate the term "gluten friendly".

Do you have a gluten horror story?
Who doesn't, we all have some stories.

What has been the biggest change since you became gluten free?
My health. I have energy, drive, motivation and I have developed a relationship with my body I never had before. I know when I need things, when I have had too much of something (sugar) and I make adjustments.

In ten years, a gluten free diet will be···
Still needed for many.

What is the best advice you received?
Read the labels and ask questions. You are your advocate.

What is the best way for people to connect with you?
My Instagram is @livingfreelyglutenfree come follow and you can DM me for any questions.

CELIAC SURVEY

We polled over 1000 people with celiac disease
with the intent to make you feel not so alone.

Should we be charged extra for a gluten free bun?

82% No

18% Yes

Presented by The 2023 Gluten Free Buyers Guide

YOU'RE NOT ALONE

Michael Frolichstein

How long have you been gluten free?

11 years

Do you have any other dietary restrictions?

No

What has been your biggest challenge thus far?

Normally, my biggest challenge would be the social gatherings which include food, but during this time of social distancing, I'm finding that I am more anxious to order food from restaurants for take-out. I am wary of getting glutened.

Where is your favorite place to eat?

I have a few, but my favorite would be Wildfire. It is a classic steakhouse style restaurant with a full gluten free menu the size of their original, and excellent protocols in place so they consistently "do it right." A nice touch is that they have our name in their system and just grab gluten free menus without us needing to ask. Plus, my wife and daughters love it, too!

Do you have any gluten related pet peeves?

My biggest pet peeve is that so many people can't wrap their minds around cross contamination. I still get strange looks and eye rolls when avoiding gluten free foods in certain situations. With The Celiac Project, I'm all about educating others, but sometimes in these personal situations I'm just frustrated and want to relax.

Do you have a gluten horror story?

Unfortunately, yes! I guess we all have at least one, and when I tell this story around my kids, they just cringe. We were making tacos and using a brand of tortillas that we thought at the time only made the corn variety. Midway through dinner my daughter, Jessica, also a celiac, commented on the taste and texture being so amazing and different than what she was used to. My wife and my eyes met in horror. I ran to the kitchen, read the package and they were wheat tortillas. I was in total disbelief at the mistake and by then it was too late. I had one of the most terrible nights of my life. So sick as a dog and I even passed out on the floor. It was the only time, to my knowledge, in the past 11 years that I knowingly consumed a gluten containing product. It was a great reminder to always double and triple check the ingredients and make no assumptions.

What has been the biggest change since you became gluten free?

Since becoming gluten free 11 years ago, the level of daily brain fog, illness, and anxiety that permeated my life since childhood dissipated, and the renewed sense of how I could redefine myself moving forward was liberating. Becoming gluten free changed more than my health, it changed the course of my life, inspiring me to start The Celiac Project-- my documentary and podcast, helping to raise awareness and bring our community together. I am very grateful for that!

In ten years, a gluten free diet will be…

…not considered a fad. My fear is that we might lose some products and restaurants, but the ones that remain will be more consistently trustworthy to the celiac and gluten intolerant community. There is also a real possibility that in ten years there will be a treatment that will hopefully allow us to not worry about cross contamination, which would be a true game-changer.

What is the best advice you received?

Stay the course. Although some people can feel better after just a couple of weeks on a gluten free diet, the majority of us take much longer to heal their gut and have their symptoms subside. This takes patience, being good to yourself emotionally when you're having a tough time because getting better is not always a straight line. Finding a good support system is also important so you don't feel alone.

What is the best way for people to connect with you?

If you would like to interact with me in a more personal way, go to www.celiacproject.com and join our Patreon #TCP Inner Circle where you can participate in a monthly live hangout with me, my podcast co-host, Cam Weiner, and our fellow community as we talk all things celiac and gluten free in an open, supportive, and positive forum. You can also email me at info@celiacproject.com and find me on Facebook, twitter or instagram @celiacproject

Chef Patrick Auger

How long have you been gluten free?

I personally changed my life to the GlutenFree community I was a professional baker for over 10 years who changed his passion to the gluten-free allergy free community

Do you have any other dietary restrictions?

Highly allergic to buckwheat flax meal .. but other than that I don't really have any allergies

What has been your biggest challenge thus far?

My biggest challenge so far is at a very young age I was diagnosed with our learning disability. Over the years I have had many mentors who have helped change my life and who have really helped me overcome my learning difference. Now I know where I meant to be in the GlutenFree allergy free community. I am very blessed to have Naomi Poe and Chef-Alina Eisenhauer as my amazing mentors in the gluten free community ..

Where is your favorite place to eat?

I can't say I really have any favorite places to eat a lot cooking and baking is done at home I'm really passionate about that hardly really go out to eat anymore

Do you have any gluten related pet peeves?

When a brand lists gluten free on their packaging and it really isn't.

What has been the biggest change since you became gluten free?

I can't say I have any challenges really. I have to say that I can eat wheat-based products and also eat gluten-free. I don't have celiac disease; I do this for the love of the gluten-free allergy free community. I found the passion in the drive to help the GlutenFree community

In ten years, a gluten free diet will be···

I'm hoping in 10 years there will be a lot more gluten-free options for the gluten-free community.

What is the best advice you received?

The best advice I received… it's from my amazing business partner Naomi Poe it's to never give up on your dream.

What is the best way for people to connect with you?

Facebook - Patrick Auger

Email - patrick.Auger12@gmail.com ..

or at https://betterbatter.org/

CELIAC SURVEY

We polled over 1000 people with celiac disease with the intent to make you feel not so alone.

What food do you miss the most?

#1 Take Out Pizza

#2 Pastries

#3 Fried Chicken

#4 Chinese Food

Presented by The 2023 Gluten Free Buyers Guide

YOU'RE NOT ALONE

Andrea Tucker

How long have you been gluten free?

10 years

Do you have any other dietary restrictions?

No

What has been your biggest challenge thus far?

Finding community and vetted sources of information. That was the motivation for starting my podcast, The Gluten Free News.

Where is your favorite place to eat?

HeartBeet Kitchen in Westmont, NJ

Do you have any gluten related pet peeves?

Products labeled gluten free that aren't.

Do you have a gluten horror story?

After many conversations at a small restaurant, my gluten free daughter found a piece of spaghetti in her salad. Needless to say, I let the manager know and have stayed far away from the establishment.

What has been the biggest change since you became gluten free?

The quality and quantity of gluten free products. The bread has gotten so much better too!

In ten years, a gluten free diet will be⋯

Well- understood and taken seriously.

What is the best advice you received?

To have a 504 plan for my daughter. It's an excellent tool for educating faculty and staff that follows her from year to year.

What is the best way for people to connect with you?

Social Media:

IG: baltimoreglutenfree FB: balimoreglutenfree Twitter: baltgf

Gluten Free Product Registration

By submitting your products into The Gluten Free Awards (GFA), you are automatically entering products into the Annual Gluten Free Buyers Guide. There are only 10 slots available in each category and we limit brands to 3 submissions per category. If you are a marketer representing multiple brands, this typically will not apply. Slots can fill quickly so we recommend submitting your registration ASAP. The absolute deadline for registration is August 22nd however, we cannot guarantee you that the category is already full.

"How do I get into the Gluten Free Awards?"

How it works:

1. Fill out the registration form by adding the quantities and product names.

(A free half page ad is given for every 5 products or full-page ad for 10 products.)

2. If wanted, add additional ad space to registration.

3. Email the registration form to Josh@GlutenFreeBuyersGuide.com

4. We will follow up with a confirmation and invoice.

If you have any questions call customer support at 828-455-9734

"Wait, I have tons of questions still"

Most common questions:

Q: I am having a hard time understanding how to submit or products.

A: Using this Registration Form will help. If lost, don't hesitate to call or email. 828-455-9734

Q: What are the image specs you need?

A: Our graphic team just needs images that are PDF, JPEG or PNG at 300 dpi or greater. The team will normally resize images based on the publishing media. Normally the product pictures and descriptions from your website will work just fine.

Full Page Ad Size 384 by 576 px

Half Page Ad Size 384 by 288 px

Q: Is there a word count for product descriptions?

A: No, we normally don't use product descriptions just product names and images.

Q: If we submit 10 products do, we get 1 free full-page ad and 2 free half page ads?

A: Sorry, please choose one or the other. You can always purchase additional ad space.

Q: Can we run a full-page ad without entering the awards program?

A: Yes.

Q: Do we need to send you product samples?

A: No. The gluten-free community votes for your products.

Q: Will we be in the guide if we don't win an award?

A: Yes, all products submitted will be visible as nominees.

Q: Can we use the GFA Nominee and Winner Badge on our product packaging, website and other related media?

A: Yes, we highly recommend using the badges to differentiate your products from the rest. If you happen to need higher resolution images don't hesitate to ask. Read our media terms here.

Need to talk about your order or have questions? Give us a call.

828-455-9734

or email

Josh@GlutenFreeBuyersGuide.com

From our family to yours, have a happy and healthy gluten free lifestyle.

The Schieffer Family

Josh (Dad with Celiac) Chief Marketing Officer

Jayme (Mom) VP Operations

Blake (22)

Jacob (18 Celiac)

Keep up to date with us, the awards, and future buyer guides at GlutenFreeBuyersGuide.com

CELIAC SURVEY

We polled over 1000 people with celiac disease
with the intent to make you feel not so alone.

Would you recommend Celiac Disease screening (blood test) for all?

68% Yes

Presented by The 2023 Gluten Free Buyers Guide

YOU'RE NOT ALONE

Notes:

Notes:

Notes:

Notes: